FINDING HOPE IN THE AXIS OF EVIL

The **Voice**
of the **Martyrs**

with Riley K. Smith

VOM
BOOKS

Iran: Finding Hope in the Axis of Evil

VOM Books
P.O. Box 443
Bartlesville, OK 74005-0443

Previously published by Living Sacrifice Books,
an imprint of The Voice of the Martyrs.

ISBN 978-0-88264-031-0

Edited by Lynn Copeland

Cover by Lookout Design

Page design and layout by Genesis Group

Printed in the United States of America

Reprinted April 2013

Unless otherwise indicated, Scripture references
are from the *New King James* version, © 1979,
1980, 1982 by Thomas Nelson Inc., Publishers,
Nashville, Tennessee.

"I cannot view Iran as the church's greatest challenge. I believe it is one of the church's 'greatest opportunities.'"

—DR. TOM WHITE, EXECUTIVE DIRECTOR,
THE VOICE OF THE MARTYRS, USA

*"The Lord stirred up the spirit of Cyrus king
of Persia, so that he made a proclamation
throughout all his kingdom, and also put it in
writing, saying, 'Thus says Cyrus king of
Persia: All the kingdoms of the earth the
LORD God of heaven has given me. And He
has commanded me to build Him a house at
Jerusalem which is in Judah. Who is among
you of all His people? May the LORD his
God be with him, and let him go up!'"*

—2 CHRONICLES 36:22,23

IRAN

CONTENTS

ACKNOWLEDGMENTS

There are several people I would like to thank who assisted in the writing of this book. Thank you to my husband who listened intently to my discoveries and challenges as I researched the book. Thank you to my mom for the interest in the subject matter and encouragement with the first draft. Thank you to those who reviewed the first draft and need to remain nameless. Thank you, Todd Nettleton, for your excellent comments and questions on the manuscript. My appreciation to my Tuesday morning Bible study group for your prayers on my writing project. Thanks to Lynn Copeland whose edits and questions made the message in this book clearer and gave me the opportunity to dig deeper and further expand my understanding of the persecuted church in Persia/ Iran. Thank you to The Voice of the Martyrs and International Antioch Ministries for your coura- geous efforts to get the gospel into Iran while en- couraging believers there, and to the many other Christian ministries that dare to reach Iran for Jesus Christ. Finally, my deepest appreciation to the Body of Christ in Iran, for risking their lives to share the most important message of hope— Jesus Christ—that an individual will ever hear.

May those who read this book be inspired to "run" (Habakkuk 2:2)!

To God be the glory!

IMPORTANT TERMS

Ashura: The holiday commemorating the martyrdom of Hussein in the seventh century. Shia Muslims will flagellate themselves using chains or whips to make themselves bleed as their way to show mourning. Some also make a pilgrimage to Karbala, in modern-day Iraq.

Ayatollah: *Aya* is Arabic for "sign of God." An ayatollah is a high-ranking authority in Shia Islam. A Muslim usually attains the status of ayatollah after completing some fete. For example, Ruhollah Khomeini achieved the rank of ayatollah after writing *The Explanation of Problems,* a book that addresses more than three thousand questions covering every aspect of Muslim life.

Basij: A grass-roots volunteer group, found in most Iranian cities, that answers to the Iranian Revolutionary Guards. This group is involved in public service through such acts as community organizing, policing morals, and suppressing protests. A *Basiji* (also spelled *Basiege*) is a member of the group.

Caliph: A leader in the Muslim world; considered a successor of Mohammed and Allah's representative on earth. The word *caliphate* is used to describe the leadership or government of the *caliph.*

Cleric: A leader and teacher in the Islamic religion. A cleric must be well-versed in the Koran and other Islamic teachings and is viewed as a guide of religious life.

Dhimma: A "protection pact" for non-Muslims in a country overtaken by Islam. In exchange for "protection" under the *dhimma*, Christians had to pay the Islamic authorities high taxes and were not allowed to proselytize, among many other stipulations. A *dhimmi* is a person provided such status under the *dhimma*.

Magi: Zoroastrian priests.

Majlis: Iran's Parliament.

Melet: A system by which Persians controlled minorities. Muslims simply adapted this concept when they invaded Persia, seeing it as a means of control.

Mobed: A Zoroastrian priest with a higher rank and qualified to teach other priests; also a term of honor for any Zoroastrian priest.

Mullah: A mullah is usually the head of a mosque, and is very knowledgeable of the Koran and other Islamic writings.

Pasdaran: Farsi for the Iranian Revolutionary Guards.

Shah: Persian for "king."

PROLOGUE:
AN ENCOUNTER WITH HOPE

They came from the East. They spotted the star and followed it. The wise men, *magi*,[1] knew that someone special, a King, had been born. As they journeyed, they made their way through Jerusalem.

"Where is the King of the Jews?" they asked. "We want to worship Him."

When King Herod heard this, he was nothing less than disturbed. *He* was the king of the Jews. He consulted with Jewish leaders about the prophecies. Sure enough, the greatest Jewish King was to be born in Bethlehem.

"Go look for this Child," he told the astrologers, "and when you find Him, tell me where He is, so I, too, can worship Him."

The men left.

The star shone ever brighter, leading the *magi* to a most unlikely place for the King of kings—not a fortress or a throne room, but a humble house.

---

1 *Magi* is also the name given to priests who follow the Zoroastrian religion. (See the sidebar on page 26 for more information.) Many Bible scholars agree that there is much uncertainty about the wise men's country of origin. The Bible says "the east." Some traditions claim they were from Persia. Marco Polo was told of their alleged burial site in Saba, Persia, when he visited Persia in the thirteenth century. Also, Persians refused to attack the Church of the Nativity (built in the fourth century) in Bethlehem in the seventh century, after the Persian attackers entered the church and saw a mosaic of three *magi* in Persian clothing.

Knowing they were in the presence of royalty, they threw themselves at Jesus' feet and worshiped Him. They had found Hope. They gave Him their gifts: gold, frankincense, and myrrh.

But before they departed, they were warned in a dream to return to their own country, which some believe was Persia, by a different way.

Today, Persians, now called Iranians, are not following a star but are drawn to the "light," other Christians, as they make their own journey toward Hope. But it's a journey that has come with a cost.

INTRODUCTION: FINDING HOPE IN THE AXIS OF EVIL

It didn't matter that he was a Sunni Muslim in Shia-dominated Iran. It didn't matter that he wasn't even ethnic Persian. What mattered was that he had turned his back on the religion of his birth —Islam—and for this, Ghorbandordi Tourani would pay with his life.

Raised as a Sunni, Ghorban wanted to study Islam in Egypt, but his father could not afford to send him. Ghorban set out to read Islamic books in his search for God, but they did not satisfy his spiritual hunger, so he turned to Marxist ideology, which, like Islam, was unfulfilling.

Like most good Muslim men, he got married. When his wife was pregnant with their third child, he left Iran for Turkmenistan in 1983 in search of work. While there, he became embroiled in an argument with another man. It became violent. Ghorban killed his aggressor with a knife and was arrested, tried, and sentenced to fifteen years in prison.

After three years in prison, Ghorban had had enough and tried to end his life. Unsuccessful, he was admitted to the prison hospital. Christian evangelists visiting the prison tried to talk with him about Christ, but he would have nothing of it. His body healed—but not his heart—and he was returned to a cell to finish out his sentence.

One day, a man named Constantine was transferred to his cell. Constantine was a believer, thrown in prison for his Christian activities. Slowly, patiently, Constantine spoke with Ghorbandordi about Christ in the squalor of their prison cell. Ghorbandordi began to show interest.

Having obtained a New Testament from the visiting evangelists, Constantine handed Ghorbandordi the book that he knew would soften his heart and give him hope. "Read this book to get to know the Jesus I share about," he told Ghorbandordi. "Then you will realize whether it is worth fighting against Him or not."

Within two weeks, Ghorban had finished reading the New Testament and was ready to place his trust in Jesus Christ.

The change in Ghorban's life was immediate and evident. Even the head of the prison noticed and gave Ghorban permission to hold evangelistic meetings. The official told him, "Because the God you worship has changed your life in such a dramatic way, I will give you permission to have meetings in the prison."

Amazed that Ghorban was allowed to hold such meetings, Constantine knew God was using Ghorban in a mighty way. "After you are released from prison, go back to Iran, to the Turkmen of your nation," he told him. "God will use you among the Turkmen in a house church meeting."

And that's exactly what Ghorban did.

After serving his fifteen-year sentence, Ghorban returned to his city of Gonbade Kavous, Iran, in 1998, and met his third child, now a teenager, for the first time. The change he had experienced after meeting Jesus was so profound that he immediately shared the gospel with friends, family, and fellow Turkmen. He boldly shared Christ in "the streets, shops, and bazaars." But his message was not always well-received. Fanatical Muslims threatened to kill him if he refused to stop sharing his faith. His own brother slashed his face with a knife. Still, many Turkmen abandoned their Muslim religion and turned to Christ.

Within two years, twelve Turkmen began meeting in his home. Ghorbandordi even sought out a Christian man in Tehran for guidance as he discipled these Muslim-background believers.

But to the Muslims of Iran, Ghorbandordi had stepped over the line. He had left Islam, was leading others astray, and had to be stopped.

On a November day in 2005, the threats against Ghorbandordi were finally carried out. Late one afternoon, he received a phone call. "I want to hear more about your beliefs. I prefer others don't see me. Can you meet me at the park in the city?"

This man had attended a meeting a week earlier where religious leaders urged Ghorban to deny Christ. After hearing Ghorban share his testimony there, perhaps the caller was genuinely interested in Christianity.

Even though Ghorban knew this could be a trap, he agreed to meet with the caller. But when he arrived at the park, the seeker was nowhere to be found. Figuring the man must have gotten scared, he walked home. At the end of an alley near his home, three people were waiting for him in a car. Within moments, Ghorban was murdered.

As they hovered over his lifeless body, his attackers shouted, "This is the punishment of those who become infidels and reject Islam!" Then they threw his body in front of his home.

When his wife, Afoul Achikeh, found him, she cried, "O people, remember that Ghorbandordi is a Christian martyr who laid down his life for the sake of Christ!"

Losing her husband wasn't the end of Afoul's ordeal. Just hours after his body was dumped, police knocked on her door, searching the home for Bibles and other Christian books in Farsi. (In Iran, it's illegal for Christians, a majority of whom are of Armenian descent, to preach in Farsi, the native language of Iran.) Secret police interrogated her and other family members under the guise of finding Ghorban's murderer. It is believed that a Turkmen terrorist group was responsible for his death.

Police crackdowns on Christians didn't stop with Ghorban's family. Iran's Ministry of Intelligence and Security (MOIS) had arrested and severely tortured ten other Christians in several other cities, including Tehran. They later released them.

Ghorbandordi Tourani, martyred in 2005

But the MOIS continued to threaten Christian leaders, giving them a warning to pass on to their fellow leaders in the house church groups: "The government knows what you are doing, and we will come for you soon."

Days before Ghorban's murder, Iran's president, Mahmoud Ahmadinejad, had told thirty provincial governors, "I will stop Christianity in this country."

Perhaps some took him seriously and decided to use Ghorban's death to send a stark message to the country: Turn from Islam and tell others to do the same, and you, too, will face death.

* * *

Ghorbandordi Tourani does not stand alone, but is on a long list of martyrs who died for the sake of Christ in the country of Iran, once known as

Persia. He joined the ranks of hundreds of thousands more who have died at the hands of fanatics attempting to make Iran a purely Zoroastrian or Shia Muslim state. The religion of the antagonists may have changed, but their zealotry has not, even being used to unify the country against an enemy when faced with external or internal strife, such as a poor economy or lack of national pride.

The following pages provide a glimpse into the persecution of Christ's Body throughout its presence in the country of Iran. Sometimes Christians were friends of Iran's shahs (Persian for "king"), and sometimes they were foes. Many faced torture, prison, and even death for refusing to turn their backs on their Savior. At times they were valiant and courageous; but there was a time when the church was marginalized, confined to its own community. Believers chose safety and survival over sharing the gospel and risking death.

Today, many Muslims in Iran—part of the "axis of evil"—are finding hope in the Person of Jesus Christ. And they're meeting Him because many are risking physical death to give Muslims the opportunity to experience eternal life.

As you read, may you refuse to let your faith become marginalized or mediocre in a world that needs to hear the hope that Jesus has to offer!

IRAN TODAY:
REJOICING IN JESUS' PRESENCE

The following letter was written by Ghorbandordi Tourani a year before he was murdered in 2005. It was mailed outside Iran.

Dear Lord Jesus, let me come to Your
presence,
So that I can touch Your nailed feet.

Dear Lord Jesus, let me worship You in
humility
And kiss Your nailed and wounded hands
and feet.

You were hung on the cross in Golgotha
and nailed with four nails, whilst Your
blood was pouring out.

In this desperate situation, how could
You still love Your created beings?
You were willing to even embrace those
who crucified You.

You were tortured because of me, yes
because of me. Not only me, but also for
my father and mother...

Because of me You suffered the most
severe pains on the cross for six hours.

I wish I was not sinful, so that You would not suffer because of me.

How much I was willing to be there and to pull the nails out of Your beautiful hands when You were on the cross.
How desperate are my thoughts when I think I might have been able to help You not to suffer a lot.

Lord Jesus, please let me glorify Your holy name in every moment of my life on this earth. I am willing to give my life that belongs to You, for the sake of You and Your church.

* * *

And that is exactly what Ghorbandordi Tourani did: He gave his life for Christ's sake and for the sake of His Body.

PERSIA'S FIRST CHRISTIANS

The sound of a roar caught their attention. Those who had come to Jerusalem from various parts of the known world focused their gaze on the wind that swirled above a building dotting the dusty streets. As they moved closer toward the cyclonic rush, they heard a murmuring. One by one, the men from many lands heard their own language.

It was the Day of Pentecost, God's initial move through the ministry of the Holy Spirit to push the gospel out into the known world.

In the Book of Acts, Luke records that on that day around three thousand placed their faith in Christ and were baptized. Among those who had witnessed the coming of the Holy Spirit were Persians from three provinces: Parthia, Media, and Elam. This was Persia's first encounter with the gospel through the ministry of the Holy Spirit. But it was decades earlier when the *magi* from the East were among the first to meet the Person of Christ. When they received word that Herod's henchmen wished to murder Baby Jesus, the *magi* "departed for their own country," which could possibly be Persia given Zoroastrianism's founding and influence there (Matthew 2:12).

History does not record an official arrival of Christianity in Persia, but some pinpoint the witness of the men from Persia on the Day of Pentecost as a likely beginning of Christianity's push into the East. Assuming these men returned to

Persia with their newfound faith, they shared the gospel in a country that claims a twenty-five-hundred-year history.

Sources also seem silent on Persia's first martyr, but a look into the accounts of the apostles' missionary assignments not long after the Day of Pentecost gives us a clue.

Tradition tells us that Simon the Zealot met up with Judas Thaddaeus in Persia, where they both met their end, with Simon facing the brutal death of being sawn in half. How ironic that God would choose to send a Jewish Zealot to an empire that would become known for its zealotry, persecuting the church at the hands of Zoroastrianism and later Shia Islam. And how ironic that a man who would be considered a terrorist by today's standards would be sent to proclaim the coming Prince of Peace in a nation that is a world leader in state-sponsored terrorism.

An Enemy of Rome is a Friend of Persia
Christianity took root and grew in Persia during the first centuries after the birth of Christ under the Parthian dynasty (ruled from 247 B.C. to A.D. 226).

Since the first century B.C., Rome and Persia were considered enemies, proving to benefit the beginnings of Christianity. In the early centuries A.D., when Rome began persecuting the church for refusing to bow and make sacrifices to their gods, Christians fled to Persia, which considered them friends since they posed a threat to their Roman rival. As Persia's Sassanid dynasty (ruled from A.D. 226 to 651) engaged the Romans in battle, pushing to the West, Christianity's influence began to spread throughout the East. Christians built monasteries that would become major outreach centers and later places of refuge under one of the most brutal persecutions that Christians would face after their relative time of peace.

But for some Persians, battling the Romans and growing their empire was not enough. Under the Sassanid dynasty, the shah, Ardashir, wanted to unify state and religion in Persia. He saw the Zoroastrian religion as the answer to his nationalistic fervor. In order to accomplish this, he appointed a Zoroastrian *mobed* (a priest, usually of a higher rank than *magi*) named Tansar, who became Ardashir's religious adviser and chief priest of the Zoroastrian clergy. The *mobeds* quickly rose in power and became highly organized. As an alleged act of loyalty to the new state religion, Ardashir destroyed some pagan temples in Armenia and in their place built fire temples for the Zoroastrians. For the first hundred years of the Sassanids, Christians were harassed by *mobeds*, but were not persecuted by the state. Not yet.

When Shah Ardashir died, his son, Shapur I, succeeded him, embracing his father's fervor for a unified state under Zoroastrianism. Tansar was succeeded by the *mobed* Kartir, who took the shah's orders a step further to strengthen the influence of Zoroastrianism behind the throne and throughout the Persian Empire.

Kartir approached his newfound position of influence with a missionary zeal to "convert the heathen and combat the foreign faiths." However, it was schisms within Zoroastrianism, such as the Manichaeans, a Gnostic religion founded by Mani, which he first targeted. When Kartir and his Zoroastrian zealots lashed out at the Manichaeans, Christians also felt the pressure. The Manichaeans used a mix of words and phrases from Christianity (as well as other religions); therefore, when they were persecuted, many Christians were also targeted due to their similarity. Not even a queen was spared. (See page 27.) Some say Christians were included in the crackdown because the Zoroastrians either could not tell the difference between the Christians and the Manichaeans, or they did not want to. Perhaps they took it out on the followers of Christ because many Manichaeans had claimed to be Christians to escape the persecution.

The Syriac *Acts of Martyrs* calls this the "first persecution" of Christians in Persia. But it would by no means be the last. Despite the persecution, Christianity would organize itself and even send a bishop, John the Persian, to the Council of Nicea in A.D. 325, to sign the creed that would make a statement against the Arian heresy. (Arianism questioned the deity of Christ by claiming that Jesus was a created being.)

Though the first centuries after Christ were relatively peaceful for Christians under the Persian Empire, where they found protection from the polytheistic Romans, this very brief encounter with persecution would be nothing like what they would face in a matter of decades.

ZOROASTRIANISM

The Zoroastrian religion was founded around the six or seventh century B.C. by Zoroaster, a prophet who claimed to see visions from a god. Zoroaster's teachings were handed down orally for centuries and later collected in a book called the *Avesta*. Followers believe in a "mystic, cosmological dualism of two warring gods in the eternal conflict"[2]—a conflict between the good god, Ahura Mazda (or Ormuzd), and the evil god of darkness, Ahriman. Those who adhere to Ahura Mazda's goodness will be rewarded with eternal life, but those possessed by the evil of Ahriman will face the "house of lies." To Zoroastrians, water and fire represent ritual purity. It is said that followers pray in the presence of fire, through which wisdom is achieved. Apparently, the *magi* of the Medes—people of Indo-Iranian ancestry living in western and northwestern present-day Iran—added aspects of a more popular religion, mixing astrology, magic, and the practice of placing the dead out in the sun. Zoroastrianism experienced a revival in Persia during the Sassanid Empire, with the aim of bringing national unity. However, when Islam invaded Persia in the seventh century, it was marginalized with few followers remaining in Iran today. Many also live in India, where they are known today as Parsees.

---

2 Moffett, *A History of Christianity in Asia, Volume I*, p. 107.

STORY FROM HISTORY:
A MARTYRED QUEEN

He was enamored with her beauty. Shah Varahran II (also known as Bahram II) was so taken by the daughter of a Byzantine[3] Roman, captured by Shapur I, that he made her his wife. But even her great beauty did not exempt her from the first persecution against Christians under this Sassanid shah who ruled from A.D. 276 to 293.

The Zoroastrian *mobed* Katir had instigated a "religious cleansing," targeting Manichaeans, whose followers had made the mistake of mixing Zoroastrianism with other religions, including Buddhism and Christianity. This was not the first time they had been attacked by the zealous Zoroastrians. But this time, Christians were caught up in the chaos.

The queen was the next to be put to death. She was brought before Varahran.

"What is your religion?" he asked.

"I am a Christian," she bravely replied. "I serve my Lord Jesus Christ, and I confess God His Father."

Her words infuriated him.

"Abandon your religion in favor of mine," he commanded. "Worship the Sun and the Fire and

---

3 "Byzantine" means "of the Byzantium Empire," which is what was left of the Roman Empire toward the end of the fourth century after it was divided.

honor the Water, and I will make you chief queen in my realm."

Perhaps the shah's demand was rooted more in fear than in anger, knowing she would die if she refused to convert to Zoroastrianism, the religion that had been fused with the throne. Regardless, she stood firm.

History and tradition tell us that she was stripped, flogged, tortured, placed in chains, and paraded naked around the city. But the crowd she drew was not one that taunted and harassed her. God's people gathered beside her. And with her face radiant and mouth filled with laughter, she faced her death.

MISSTEPS AND MASSACRE: THE GREAT PERSECUTION (A.D. 340–401)

Their fate was sealed when the shah received a letter and a careless prophecy. For more than two hundred years, Persia's Christians had been protected by the shahs, and given refuge from the Romans who were persecuting God's people. Though they had previously faced brief opposition during a Zoroastrian crackdown on heretics, they remained strong in the Lord, even organizing themselves into a body of believers with an administrative structure. But their foundation would soon be shaken by an unprecedented persecution that would send tens of thousands to their death.

Constantine's Letter and Aphrahat's Prophecy

The dominion of polytheistic emperors came to an end when Constantine embraced Christianity and issued the Edict of Milan, ending centuries of Christian persecution. But now that Christians were a friend to Rome—Persia's rival—they came under the shah's suspicion in Persia.

In a well-meaning attempt to help Christians in Persia, Constantine sent a letter to the shah, Shapur II (ruling from 309 to 379), around the year 315. "I rejoice to hear that the fairest provinces of Persia are adorned with Christians," he wrote. "Since you are so powerful and pious, I commend them to your care, and leave them to your protection." Another historian says that Constantine wrote, "There is nothing in their religion of a reprehensible nature."

What Constantine viewed as a gesture to guarantee further protection of the people who professed his newfound faith, the shah saw as suspect.

It didn't help matters that two decades later, Shapur II received word that Constantine was amassing his army to battle the East, reinforcing his distrust of Rome and their new friends, the Christians. But it was a Persian preacher named Aphrahat who unwisely predicted a Roman victory over Persia after reading Old Testament prophecy.

Shapur II was incensed, but it would be a matter of years before his anger would be unleashed on the Christians.

In 337, Constantine died and split the empire among his three sons. Seeing an opportunity to defeat his enemy once and for all, Shapur II led his men to attack the walled city of Nisibis. Though their emperor was dead, the Romans' resolve and discipline were not. Shapur II's men withdrew.

The Whisper
"There is no secret which [Bishop] Simon[4] does not write to Caesar to reveal," whispered the Zoroastrians in the ear of Shapur II. Unable to defeat

---

4 Simon was the bishop of Seleucia-Ctesiphon, the church's base of operations.

the Romans at Nisibis, Shapur took action against what he would consider the Romans' proxies—Christians.

Shapur II's first line of attack came in the form of imposing a double tax on Christians and holding Bishop Simon responsible for collecting it. The shah called for Simon to be arrested, and decreed, "You will not release him until he has signed this document and agreed to collect the payment to us of a double tax and a double tribute for all the [Christians]."

Knowing the Christians would come short of paying the tax, Simon appealed to the shah. "I am no collector but a shepherd of the Lord's flock," he said.

But the shah was not finished with the Christians. With the support of the zealous Zoroastrian *mobeds*, he issued a second decree: the destruction of churches and the execution of clergy who refused to participate in the national worship of the sun.

Again, Simon was arrested and brought before the shah, who offered him gifts in exchange for worshiping the sun. Simon refused. He was then promised that if he alone would turn his back on Christianity, his people would not be harmed. But if Simon refused, he would be condemning not just the church leaders, but all Christians. The Christians who were present were furious and rose up in indignation at such an outrageous proposal.

The shah and his band of *mobeds* responded swiftly and ordered Simon and church leaders to their death. On Good Friday, in the year 344, he along with five bishops and one hundred priests were led outside the city of Susa. One by one Simon witnessed their beheading. Finally it was his turn to be martyred for refusing to turn his back on Christ.

This murderous act sparked a systematic persecution of the church. Christians were tracked down in every corner of the Persian Empire. One source says that it was at times a general massacre but more often an "intensive organized elimination of the church leadership."

However, the shah was not finished with his wave of violence. He issued a third decree, targeting Christians who had converted from Zoroastrianism. The *mobeds* carried out the martyrdoms, and Christians began suspecting the Jews of being informants. The Zoroastrians' hatred of Christians intensified. "The Christians destroy our holy teachings," they complained, "and teach men to serve one God, and not to honor the sun or fire."

The martyrdom of Simon and the great number of Christians shook the organization of the church. As soon as a new bishop was appointed, he too was killed. When an eighty-year-old bishop named Qayuma was asked to take on the role as leader of the church, he responded, "I am going to die soon anyway, and I had rather die as a martyr than of old age."

Persecution finally decreased in intensity prior to Shapur II's death in 379. Some wonder if he had issued a decree of toleration or if his victory against the Romans (Julian) had helped to ease his hatred. Regardless, a succession of weaker shahs with bigger problems graced the Persian throne. With feudal underlords within their borders and the White Huns from central Asia threatening their northern border, the shah's and Zoroastrians' anger might have been redirected toward larger issues endangering the empire and finally led them to end the Great Persecution around the year 401.

By then, tremendous damage had been done. Church historian Sozomen wrote that the number of martyrs was incalculable, and another source estimates as high as 190,000. Persia's Great Persecution was worse than anything Christians endured under the Romans, including Diocletian, under whom it was said that more church leaders were in prison than actual criminals. However, the glimmer of hope was the steadfast faith of Persia's Christians during this time of systematic violence. Though the church's organization had been shaken, it would recover just in time to face a new challenge: confinement to a community and a split that would divide the church between the East and the West for centuries.

A CHURCH RECOVERED … THEN CONFINED (4ᵀᴴ–7ᵀᴴ CENTURIES)

The fourth century was coming to a close, and the White Huns had broken through Persia's northern border, forcing Persia to shift its focus from its old Roman rivals to the barbarians to the north. In the meantime, the church recovered after losing almost two hundred thousand believers in the Great Persecution. But with its troubles far from over, the church would experience a series of victories and setbacks leading it into an era that would change the face and force of the nation for more than a millennium.

In 409, Shah Yazdegerd issued an edict of toleration toward the church. As significant as Constantine's Edict of Milan in 313, this decree officially ended the persecution of Christians. The shah even tried his hand at church politics, going so far as appointing someone to the highest position of leadership in the church and calling him "Chief of all the Christians of the Orient." But peace for the Christians was fleeting. The Zoroastrians would never forgive the shah for this gesture of tolerance, and as the Zoroastrians' fanaticism and the feudal lords' restlessness increased, the shah soon shifted back to viewing Christians as a liability.

A Zoroastrian high priest approached the shah with concerns about the high number of converts to Christianity. It did not help matters that Christians were burning down Zoroastrian fire temples in the empire. Knowing that his security as shah rested somewhat in the hands of the *mobeds*, the shah allowed them to persuade converts to return to the national religion, "not, however, by death, but by fear and a certain amount of beating."

After Yazdegerd died, he was succeeded by Varahran V (reigning from 421 to 439), who issued a nationwide campaign against Christians. He even went so far as demanding that the Byzantine emperor, Theodosius II, deny sanctuary to Christians fleeing persecution in Persia and return the fugitives. Theodosius was so offended by the shah's audacity in making such a demand that he launched an attack on Persia, leading to an indeterminate war that lasted for months, which did not help matters for Persia's Christians.

Varahran V's successor, Yazdegerd II (reigning from 439 to 457), continued persecuting the church, even opening his reign by declaring war on Byzantium. During his reign, a horrific persecution occurred, nearly rivaling the Great Persecution in the number of martyrs.

In 448, at Kirkuk (in modern-day Iraq), tens of thousands of Christians were hauled to a mound outside the city and slaughtered for days. More than one hundred fifty thousand bishops, clergy, and laypeople were among those martyred. But their death did not prove in vain. The chief persecutor, Tamasgerd, was so stirred by the steadfastness of these believers that he placed his faith in the Christ they were dying for and joined them in death. Local tradition claims that the red gravel on this small hill was stained by the martyrs' blood.

Despite the mass killings and witch hunt to reconvert Zoroastrian-background believers, the Persian church sent missionaries to the East, taking with them the gospel.

A Church Marginalized and a
Patriarch Under Pressure

Under Shah Chosroes I (reigning from 531 to 579), Christians faced a new dilemma called the *melet*. Alarmed by the growth of Christianity, the *mobeds* viewed this system as a way to stem that growth. Under the *melet*, Persia controlled Christians by granting them limited freedoms to organize themselves and worship, reducing them to second-class status under Zoroastrians. Some believe that Christians were forced to dress in a certain way as proof of conformance to the *melet*. Despite these limitations, the church continued to grow in influence and wealth, arousing more jealousy among the *mobeds*.

During this time, a church leader named Mar Aba was targeted by Zoroastrians in their campaign to reconvert those who turned to Christianity.

Patriarch of Persia's church, Mar Aba had previously been a follower of Zoroastrianism. His popularity was great among the people, and the *mobeds* wanted to stop him before he persuaded others to join him and convert to Christianity.

The leader of the *mobeds* finally brought charges before the shah. Not only had Mar Aba converted from Zoroastrianism, he had also persuaded others to convert, and condemned Persians who promoted and practiced marriage between close relatives.

Arrested and brought before the shah, Mar Aba made his defense. "I am a Christian," he said. "I preach my own faith, and I want every man to join it."

The shah tried to convince him to stop receiving converts among other issues he disagreed with, but Mar Aba refused. Pronounced guilty, Mar Aba was sent to prison. Then after the drama

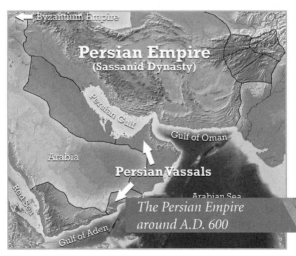

The Persian Empire around A.D. 600

of his case had calmed, the shah sentenced him to exile. But exile was not enough for the zealous Zoroastrians. Because he was still able to govern the church and his administration had apparently strengthened, they tried to assassinate him.

Breaking his exile, Mar Aba appeared before the shah to protest the assassination attempts, and the Zoroastrians tried to kill him on the spot. However, the Christians accompanying Mar Aba surrounded him for protection. Mar Aba was sent back to prison.

Unsuccessful at restricting the church through the *melet* and the exile of an influential leader, Chosroes I decided to control it by appointing patriarchs. When Chosroes II came to the throne (reigning from 590 to 628), he brought with him a Nestorian[5] wife. Though he built churches, he still warred with the Byzantine Empire, draining the Persian Empire's army and resources so dry that they would prove unable to withstand a new rival: Arab Muslims from the south.

---

5 The fifth century witnessed a division in the church that created a rift between the churches in the East and West. It began when a theologian named Nestorius criticized a well-known religious expression, erupting into a conflict regarding Christ the person and Christ the divine. Nestorius was condemned for his beliefs at the Council of Ephesus in A.D. 431. Adding to the controversy surrounding Nestorius's statements was his claim that he rejected the divine nature of Christ ("God the Word") as capable of suffering. Nestorian Christians are those who aligned themselves with Nestorius.

IRAN TODAY:
A DAUGHTER IN HIDING

She turned her back on Islam—the faith she was born into—and chose instead to follow Christ. "Delilah," just a youth, would face serious consequences for such a "treasonous" act in her country of Iran.

Her father discovered her betrayal to their religion and, furious, he attempted to straighten out his infidel daughter. At knife-point, he forced her to recite the Muslim prayers. As Delilah dutifully delivered what her father wanted to hear, she quietly prayed to her heavenly Father in her heart.

But her father's rage did not deter her from pursuing Jesus. She got hold of a Gospel. Fearing for her life, she carefully tore out pages of the Scriptures and hid them in her clothing, taking them out to read whenever she was alone.

One day Delilah's mother discovered the pages and told her father. Without showing any mercy, he beat Delilah and planned to do what many Muslim fathers have done in that situation: marry her off to a Muslim man to seal her fate—and faith—for good.

Delilah heard about her father's plan and ran away. She called her father, pleading with him not to be angry, but he had endured enough shame. "Your sin will only be forgiven," he said, "if your blood is shed."

There was now only one Father she could turn to, one who would not reject her—her heavenly Father.

Delilah wanted to live. She went into hiding where she is committed to sharing her testimony with others, so they can meet the One who shed His blood for the sins of all mankind.

THE ARAB INVASION: THE RISE OF ISLAM (7TH–15TH CENTURIES)

They came from the desert sands in the south. Little attention was paid to the Arab invaders whose Bedouin tribes would be united by a religion founded by a man named Mohammed. The Persian Empire was so embroiled in its own battles with Byzantium that it failed to prepare for the invasion that would change the empire for centuries to come.

Muslims conquered the Persian Empire in 636, bringing an end to the Sassanid dynasty, which taxed its people so heavily to support its excessive lifestyle that few would defend it from the Arab invaders. Even the Nestorian Christians initially perceived the Arabs as quasi-liberators from their Zoroastrian persecutors. This was not the case. Arabs attempted to force Islam on the people, creating a rift between Arabs and Persians that remains today.

Needing a structure to control the conquered Persians, the Arabs developed what became known as the Covenant of Umar, or the Pact of Umar (or Omar), a set of decrees that dictated how non-Muslims would be governed. Some say that the covenant "turned Islam from an army of unified Arab tribes to an empire."

Arab Muslims retained the Sassanid's *melet* —a system controlling Christians, Jews, and now

Zoroastrians—but under Islam it was called the *dhimma*, a pact to "protect" followers of these religions.

Christians welcomed some of the changes, such as not being allowed to serve in the army. They were limited to certain occupational positions, like physicians, merchants, and farmers, and were still burdened with a heavy tax called a *jizya*, which brought in high revenues to support the Arab military and maintain its standard of living. In exchange for the "privilege" of living under the *dhimma*, all non-Muslims were required to pay this tax, which could rightfully be called "protection money." To avoid paying the high taxes, many either fled to the hills or converted to Islam.

Alarmed at the loss of revenue from the high number of fugitives and converts to Islam, the Arabs took action to ensure their fiscal livelihood. They ordered a census and issued passes to those who registered and paid their taxes. Like a passport, the pass was required—anyone caught without their paper was put to death. Used as late as the Middle Ages, this practice developed into the requirement for non-Muslims to wear the tax receipt around their neck or a seal on their wrist or chest. Some accounts relate the practice of attempting to humiliate *dhimmi* (those who lived under the *dhimma*) by forcing them to pay their tax in public while Muslims struck them on the head or neck.

The requirements for Christians were not limited to paying taxes; the law even dictated how a non-Muslim was to dress. In some places, Christians were ordered to wear a particular type of girdle around their waist to set them apart from the Arabs. Later, a large yellow patch was worn on their outer garments (eerily prophetic of the Star of David that Jews would be forced to wear in Nazi Germany). Christians were required to have a special haircut with the front shaved, to ride horses side-saddle, and to ride on the sides of the road—the center was reserved for Muslims. Non-Muslims were given some representation with the *caliphs* (Muslim rulers), but it was limited in scope and was more of an illusion of having a voice in the government.

The most debilitating strike against the church in the Covenant of Umar was the prohibition against the conversion of Muslims. Slowly but steadily, the church faded, choosing survival and physical safety over thriving and physical suffering for the sake of the gospel.

Persecution did continue but in other forms. During the eighth century, construction of church buildings was forbidden, and any new constructions had to be demolished. Christians were being pushed further and further down the social ladder, while the church decayed internally through bribery and greed. The *dhimma* was having the desired effect on the church. Many Christians aspired to high positions in government and education, and those who had much wealth found it being consumed by the *dhimma*'s high taxes. Many even converted to Islam in order to avoid paying the high taxes (or facing death for refusing to pay), which alarmed the Muslims when they saw their source of monetary gain dwindle. Christians were abandoning Christ's Great Commission for the sake of their wealth. As one Christian said, "The monks are no longer really missionaries."

While the Arabs were dealing with their own internal conflicts that splintered their religion (see the sidebar on page 46), Persia would face another foreign invasion—this time from the Mongols from the East—and the arrival of Catholic missionaries.[6]

In the thirteenth century, the Mongols attacked Persia, and Islam remained unaffected. The seventh *ilkhan* ("subordinate khan") named Ghazan (ruling from 1295 to 1304) converted to Islam from Buddhism. In what appeared to be a gesture of loyalty to his newfound faith, Ghazan almost immediately decreed the destruction of churches, synagogues, and Buddhist temples. He eventually put an end to this persecution when he discovered that his general, a Muslim named Naurez who was instrumental in Ghazan's conversion to Islam, had plotted against Persia with Muslim Egypt. Naurez's fanaticism fueled the persecution against the Christians, some of which

---

6 Some Nestorians unified with the Catholic Church and become the Chaldean Church.

was motivated by greed, as he hoped to benefit from the Christians' wealth. Naurez was executed, and Christians celebrated,

Succeeding Ghazan were a series of Mongol emperors who continued his tradition of persecuting the church.

The brutal Mongol emperor Tamerlane was unable to keep Persia unified. In 1499, the Persians took back their throne with the Safavid dynasty (ruling until 1736). The Mongol invaders were ousted, but once again Islam was not.

Even though Christians were liberated from yet another oppressor, the Safavids continued to persecute the church. The church's organization was crumbling. Several hundred more years would pass before a Persian shah would remove the *dhimma* discrimination that had a crippling effect on the church. Until then, the Nestorians were isolated, their vigor and resolve dying under the *dhimma*. They embraced survival and safety over evangelization and risk, trying to avoid the inevitable conflict. They were no longer able to read the ancient Syriac language, as it had developed into a modern Syriac, and therefore could not read vital literature, such as the Scriptures, that could have strengthened their faith during these troubling times. In addition, Nestorian traditions were not passed down to the next generation.

Protestant missions would soon arrive in Persia, but was it too late to help the besieged body of believers?

SUNNIS AND SHIA

The prophet Mohammed died in 632, without naming a successor to be the next *caliph*, or leader, of Islam. Arabia's tribal culture knew two models for selecting a leader: bloodlines or consensus. Since Mohammed had left behind only daughters and no sons, his son-in-law Ali seemed the logical choice, but he was overlooked in favor of Abu Bakr, Mohammed's closest confidante. To prevent a dispute, Abu Bakr instead named Umar as *caliph*. Discontentment grew among Ali's followers. Umar was murdered, and again someone else was appointed *caliph*—Uthman.

Muslims began taking sides, with those following Ali being called *Shia Ali* (followers of Ali), or *Shi'ites* (party of Ali). They embraced the idea that Islam's leaders should come from "the Prophet's house," whereas Sunnis believed they should be selected by consensus. The conflict continued. Uthman was murdered, and Ali was finally appointed *caliph*. His position ended after only five years when he was assassinated. But one of his sons, Hussein, vowed to avenge his death.

Nineteen years later, Hussein and a band of seventy-two men, women, and children confronted the Umayyids (ruling Muslims) at Karbala (in present-day Iraq). But Hussein's party was no match for the Umayyids. Hussein and his companions were slaughtered. To this day, Karbala is a holy city for the Shia, who commemorate the death of Hussein and his followers by observing a holiday called Ashura and praying to them.

Hussein's death would solidify the rift between Sunnis and Shia, giving credence to the act of martyrdom as a means to serve Allah. Several centuries would pass before Persia became primarily Shia. Today, ninety percent of all Muslims are Sunnis, and ten percent are Shia, a majority of whom live in modern-day Iran. Ninety-three percent of Iranians are Shia Muslims.

PROTESTANT MISSIONS IN PERSIA (18TH–19TH CENTURIES)

They began to pack up and leave. Having arrived in Persia five hundred years earlier (their second era of missions there), Catholic missionaries were departing by the eighteenth century. Their plan to convert the Nestorians to Catholicism was not working. As Nestorians traded one set of liturgies for another, they found themselves out from under the protection of the *dhimma*, which didn't cover Catholics.

But as Catholic missionaries left, Protestant missionaries arrived. Two Moravian German Protestants named Hoecker and Rueffer arrived in the mid-eighteenth century; however, their short stint in Persia would be riddled with robberies and illness.

With professions in medicine, the men started their journey to the East traveling with a caravan of about fifteen hundred camels in through the desert. When they came to the first Persian town, they were advised to stay awhile, as the road ahead was filled with bandits. Three weeks later they set out again, but the bandits were still there. With a much smaller caravan, they had not traveled far before two hundred Kurdish bandits attacked them. After only two shots, the horsemen in their caravan were spooked and fled, leaving those who remained an easy target.

Hoecker and Rueffer were wounded, losing all their clothes to the carousing Kurds. In the blazing heat, the two walked fifteen miles to the next town, where a Persian gave them a place to stay, as well as some food and clothing.

After resting a few days, they set back out on their journey but were once again robbed. This time one was left with his trousers and the other his waistcoat. They had little food left and were grateful to find shelter in stables along the way.

When they finally reached the city of Isfahan, they were guests of an English resident, who persuaded the men to stay awhile before they set out for Gaures. They stayed six months. In 1748, they left Isfahan but had not traveled far until they were robbed once again. Rueffer's health suffered terribly from the long ordeal. He died, and Hoecker returned to Europe.

Other Protestant missionaries would arrive, one being Henry Martyn. Initially a chaplain to India, Martyn was particularly gifted in learning new languages. While striving to bring the gospel to Hindus and Muslims in India, Martyn translated the New Testament into Urdu (the official language of Pakistan today) and Farsi (or Persian). Wanting to improve his translation, he went to Persia in 1811. But he died within the year, unable to fulfill his dream of giving the shah a copy of the Bible. With the help of the British Ambassador, a copy finally did reach the shah, who promised to read it.

Missions to the Nestorians

More than twenty years after Martyn's death, Justin Perkins of the United States arrived in Persia. Thinking he had found a group of pre-Reformation Protestants, he had really found the Nestorians who welcomed this man of faith. Perkins was troubled to learn the Nestorians were primarily illiterate, unable to read their own language, which was a modern version of ancient Syriac. No one had committed it to writing. It was different enough from the ancient Syriac that reading their ancient literature was impossible. They had no printed books and no Bible to tell them that persecution for Christ was normal. No wonder the Nestorians had slowly drifted into stagnation and settled for the opportunity to "survive" under the *dhimma*.

Since the American foreign mission board had mandated that missionaries evangelize the Muslim world by reforming the ancient churches of the East (like the Nestorians), equipping them to reach out to their Muslim neighbors, Perkins knew what he needed to do. With the help of a Nestorian church leader named Abraham, Perkins diligently created a written language from the modern Syriac. Soon, the first printing press arrived, clicking off copies of the Bible and later other pieces of Christian literature like John Bunyan's *Pilgrim's Progress* and numerous theological tracts and stories.

But the work of Perkins and other Protestant missionaries did not go unnoticed or unopposed. Revival was occurring among the Nestorians, but it added to the already apparent conflict. The Nestorians' long and incomprehensible liturgies were at odds with the simple congregational worship brought over by the Protestant missionaries. Villagers were confused by the differences between the traditional Nestorians and those Nestorians who were evangelized by Protestant missionaries. Church life between the two distinctive groups was also tense. Some patriarchs saw the excitement over the message that Protestant missions had brought as a threat to their authority. One Nestorian patriarch was so infuriated that he had his men beat a Nestorian priest, leading to a rebellion. The shah's son intervened, ordering an end to the violence, but the damage was done. The conflict between Nestorian and Protestants hurt their Christian witness among Muslims.

By the close of the nineteenth century, the Ottoman Empire was falling apart. Having taken root almost six hundred years earlier with a broad reach from parts of Europe to the East, the Ottomans' days were numbered. The Middle East remained Muslim, but it was turning against vulnerable ethnic minorities, like the Armenians across the border in Turkey. (See page 53.) The impact that Protestant missions had made was small compared to Islam. One church historian wrote of the Nestorians, "A conviction had grown that the organization of the ancient Church could not be thoroughly reformed in the evangelical spirit; that its services could not be adapted to modern needs; that there would ever be a remnant of the old half-heathenish leaven."

But not all was lost. Protestant missions' most passionate converts were the Nestorian women. One source tells the story of a Muslim governor's reaction to a group of women who had gathered to celebrate the fiftieth anniversary of Protestant work and had been taught to read by the missionaries.

"What are these women doing with books in their hands?" asked the Muslim governor.

"They are reading and singing."

"Impossible."

When the women were asked to stand if they could read, six hundred rose to their feet. The Muslim governor was astonished, as he could not believe that women were capable of learning to read.

During the nineteenth century, Protestant missions did not have the renaissance in Persia and the Middle East that it had experienced in nations farther east, such as China. But in the spirit of optimism, the missionaries still planted seeds. Those seeds would take root and grow during the next several decades to prepare the country for what could be one of the most fanatical regimes witnessed in the twentieth century.

STORY FROM HISTORY:
THE ARMENIAN MASSACRE

They were considered "reached," having received and embraced the gospel as early as the fourth century. Credited as having "the oldest organized Christian community in the world," Armenians had struggled for their own independent nation, with many living in countries such as Persia. Over time, the Armenian church had grown stagnant. That would soon change, followed by a fierce opposition that would lead to a holocaust.

Protestant evangelical missionaries brought the gospel to the Armenians in the nineteenth century, triggering a revival within the old Armenian church. Becoming troubled at the vast numbers turning to this evangelical view of Christianity, an Armenian church leader banned Bibles and books that the missionaries had imported and then had several evangelical Armenian leaders imprisoned.

Armenians were under a Turkish Muslim government (the Ottoman Empire), where conversion of a Muslim to Christianity was punishable by death. Then in 1856, this law was lifted, and a number of Muslims became Christians. However, this religious freedom was brief, as eight years later, the Turkish government imprisoned Muslim converts to Christianity.

Fearing an Armenian uprising, Turkish government soldiers killed up to one hundred thousand Armenians from 1895 to 1896. One source says ten thousand of them were evangelical Protestants. Villages were looted and churches destroyed. A leader of the old Armenian church refused to convert to Islam. For this, his hands and then lower arms were cut off, and finally he was decapitated.

Then in 1915, as the Ottoman Empire was losing power and influence, the Turks accused the Armenians of assisting Russian invaders and unleashed an act of genocide murdering an estimated six hundred thousand—three times the number of victims in Persia's Great Persecution in the fourth century. Working professionals, church leaders, and others were captured and charged with treason. Heads were placed in vises and squeezed until the victims collapsed. Thousands of children were pushed alive into ditches and buried. Others were stoned. Some were branded on the chest and back with red-hot iron crosses. Women and girls were raped before they were murdered.

Neither evangelicals nor members of the established church were exempt from the slaughter. The Armenians who escaped the Turkish soldiers fled into the desert, where many died. Only the strongest escaped into Russian territory.

Pockets of Armenians are still found in what remains of the Russian, Turkish, and Persian (Iranian) Empires. Today in Iran, Christians are primarily of Armenian descent. Pastors are allowed to preach only in Armenian and anyone caught using Farsi to communicate Christian truths—or worse, to lead a Muslim to Christ—is severely punished. During the 1990s, several Armenian pastors in Iran would face such a harsh penalty, even paying with their lives.

REVOLUTIONARY FURY: MULLAHS VERSUS MODERNIZATION (1900-1953)

For centuries Persia had defended itself against the wiles of the West, first with the Romans, then the Byzantines and Ottomans, and now with Europe. The West—with all its cultural, financial, and political temptations to modernize—was knocking on Persia's door, threatening the Shia hierarchy's goal of maintaining its Islamic past and traditions, and even more, of preserving its power over the people. And that power would affect the church.

During the first half of the twentieth century, Persia faced a series of revolutions that would one day lead to the Islamic Revolution of 1979. Each uprising created nothing less than an iron-fisted shah that demanded modernization while selling Iran's soul to foreigners, infuriating not only the Shia Muslims, but also the secularists.

Power to the People or More to the Shah?
The Constitutional Revolution in the early 1900s was fueled in the previous century by Shah Nasir ed-Din, when he granted more rights to foreigners. Around 1891, he sold the country's entire tobacco crop to the British Imperial Tobacco Company for 15,000 British pounds a year—money that he used to support his excessive lifestyle. Shia leaders felt such an exchange sub-

jected Iran's Shia to European values and ideals. The people were furious and protested, and the shah fell victim to an assassin.

Nasir ed-Din's oldest son, Muzaffar, took the throne and the people revolted, insisting on balanced political power through a parliament. The shah finally agreed to establish a parliament and write a constitution, limiting the shah's power while giving more control to the people. In addition to opposing the foreign sell-out, a portion of Persia believed in guaranteeing equal rights under the law to non-Shia, such as Christians, Sunni Muslims, and Zoroastrians. This did not set well with the Shia, who felt such a gesture gave minorities too much power and threatened the Shia's exalted position over the masses.

As promised, the shah gave the people a parliament, called the *Majlis*. But time would prove that giving more power to the people through a parliament would not produce a modern state. It merely became a breeding ground for more resentment toward the West's presence and perceived economic domination. This would prove fatal for the country in the following decades.

A Fanatical Push Toward Modernization Backfires

The year 1925 introduced Persia's newest leader, Reza Shah. Committed to Westernization, Reza saw Shia leaders as the primary stumbling block to his vision of a progressive Persia and held them

Reza Shah

solely responsible for the country's lack of growth and modernization. Instead of using a more democratic or diplomatic approach, he chose to enact policies inhibiting the power of Shia mullahs.

Wanting to erase Persia's primitive perception in the world, Reza mandated Western-style dress. He prohibited women from wearing a *chador*, or veil in public. To Muslims, the veil was a symbol of modesty, but to Reza's reformers it was a symbol of the old subordinate status of women. He also restricted wearing of the turban and cloak to men who were knowledgeable in the law. Judges were now required to obtain a law degree from a secular university, preventing them from using only the Koran and Islamic tradition to interpret the law. He pushed for a national railroad and closed all schools run by Muslims, Christians, and other minority religions, and required that both boys and girls obtain a free education through the state. Foreigners visiting the ancient nation were not allowed to take photographs of camels, as they reinforced Persia's primitive past.

Reza continued his attacks on the Shia by making religious leaders look like they represented the old Persia. Knowing Shia Islam had rallied the citizens of his country, Reza had to enact a new unifying force or his days would be numbered. So he decided to link Persia to its pre-Islamic past and tried to revitalize Zoroastrianism. In 1935, he changed the country's name to Iran.

Still attempting to break Islam's hold over the nation, Reza disrupted the mullahs' financial status by taking the substantial revenue from the shrines and committing mullahs to two years of military service. He targeted the Shia holiday of Ashura by banning the holiday's dramatic reenactment of the martyrdom of Hussein and prohibiting self-flagellation. Since he had banned the veil from society, policemen were sent out onto the streets to seize scarves off women's heads. Educated women welcomed the new freedoms, but many opposed this ban, saying it made them feel disgraced. To them, the veil was a symbol of modesty, not something to be sacrificed on the altar of modernity. Men were required to wear the Pahlavi hat, which prevented them from touching their forehead to the ground during prayers.

Meanwhile, long aware that Iran was sitting on oil, Great Britain continued to pressure the shah for concessions. Great Britain won when given control over extracting and managing the "liquid gold," and was even allowed to set the price.

Reza's fanatical push toward Westernization came to an end when he decided to call upon

Mohammad Reza Shah

Nazi Germany as a third foreign force in Iran, in addition to Great Britain and the Soviet Union were two existing foreign influences in Iran.) Britain and Russia reacted by shutting down the railroad Reza had worked so hard to have constructed. Reza resigned in 1941, and Britain and Russia selected his son, Mohammed Reza, to take his place.

A Rogue Prime Minister and the Evil CIA

Mohammed Reza Shah reversed many of his father's fanatical policies against Shia Islam. He made it acceptable for women to wear the veil in public and allowed the Shia play during Ashura as well as pilgrimages to Shia holy sites. But as the new shah was winning favor among the Shia, a charismatic figure rose from the parliament and challenged his leadership.

Muhammed Mossadeq was elected prime minister in 1951 and made his life's purpose very clear: oust the Brits. Perceiving Britain to be a "nation of satanically clever manipulators intent on plundering Iran, ... [he] led villagers to believe with certainty that locusts, drought and crop failure resulted from nothing less than the evil designs of the British."[7]

He successfully drove out Britain's Anglo-Iranian Oil Company but was left with a bigger problem: he had not a clue how to run the oil business. Iranians were not trained to manage the extraction and exportation of oil. Ultimately, oil exports dropped and so did Iran's income.

So what did Mossadeq do? He turned to a foreign government for help—the United States. In the process of Mossedeq's crusade to rid the country of the Brits, Mohammed Reza Shah was pushed aside and left Iran. In an ironic turn of events, he, too, sought the United States for help. During the summer of 1953, Allen Dulles (head of the CIA), Loy Henderson (U.S. ambassador to Iran) and Princess Ashraf (Mohammed Reza Shah's twin sister) appeared in Switzerland, apparently as part of a plot to oust the problematic Prime Minister Mossadeq.

Muhammed Mossadeq

Soon after the historic meeting, Mohammed Reza Shah returned to Iran to reclaim his throne,

---

7 Mackey, p. 194.

and Mossadeq was put on public trial and ousted from his position in 1953.

The accusations started to fly.

Suspecting the United States was behind having Mossadeq forced out, Iran labeled the U.S. Embassy in Tehran as a "nest of spies," and "CIA" would become a derogatory term in the minds of both Shia and secularists in Iran. This was a turning point in Iran's view of the United States and the West. Britain was the evil occupying force thrown out, while the U.S. was the puppet master controlling Iran to maintain its own superpower status in the world. Decades later, fanatical students would take revenge on the U.S. Embassy in Tehran.

These events fueled the fury of an ayatollah named Ruhollah Khomeini, who in a matter of decades would prove to the world that a purely Shia Islamic state was more than a possibility. He would make it a reality.

END OF THE SHAH, RISE OF THE AYATOLLAH (1960s-1980)

He emerged as a dark, looming figure who gave a voice to decades of anger and resentment. With his message accusing the shah of leading Iran unjustly and calling for him to step down, Ayatollah Ruhollah Khomeini unified Iran and became the man who would lead the country into a revolution that changed Iran and its standing in the world.

Ruhollah Khomeini was born to parents who claimed direct descent from the Prophet Mohammed, but Khomeini's father would never have the chance to see his son rise in the ranks of Shia leadership. As chief mullah of their village (Khomein), Khomeini's father had a man executed for breaking the fast during the Muslim holy month of Ramadan, when Muslims are required to fast from sunup to sundown. He was murdered when a friend of the man who was executed took revenge. His mother and aunt raised him.

Khomeini received the status of "Ayatollah" after publishing *The Explanation of Problems*, a book that addresses more than three thousand questions for the Shia Muslim, ranging from how to use the bathroom properly to dealing with oppressive rulers. But it was in the early 1960s that Khomeini's voice was heard and soon embraced among the Iranian people, beginning with Mohammed Reza Shah's land reforms.

The shah purchased land from wealthy owners and resold it to peasants at reasonable rates. At the time, land was also a means of power; therefore, the shah's action challenged the reigning aristocracy and Shia clergy who lashed out at the shah. But the shah didn't stop at empowering people through land ownership; he also tried to improve society through healthcare and giving

Ayatollah Ruhollah Khomeini

women the right to vote. Khomeini reacted to the reforms and denounced them as "un-Islamic." The shah shot back, calling the Shia clergy "black reactionaries," fueling further tension in the country. To control the clergy's influence, the shah ordered more than sixty mullahs into detention, required seminary students to report to the military, and restricted government funds to the clergy. He also tightened security around Qom, the city that housed the theological institute where Khomeini studied, lectured, and launched his opposition to the shah.

Sensing the growing turmoil, the shah ordered the military to raid the theological school in Qom, killing two and arresting dozens of students. Those who escaped ran to Khomeini.

Khomeini led mourning ceremonies for those slain in the raid, but the shah ordered the electricity to the city to be cut off. Prepared for such a drastic response, Khomeini's men uncovered a generator and resumed the ceremony. Khomeini was arrested but later released.

Prison did not intimidate Khomeini into silence. It only served to deepen his resolve and expand his influence among the people as opportunities arose to criticize the shah. But Khomeini's days in Iran would soon be numbered.

Lyndon B. Johnson, then President of the United States, offered the shah $200 million in military equipment and access to U.S. military advisers, with one condition: that the shah sign the Status of Forces Agreement (SOFA), which allowed Americans who committed crimes in Iran to be tried in the United States. Khomeini was furious, denouncing it as a "document of enslavement" and condemning the president, saying, "Let the American president know that in the eyes of the Iranian people, he is the most repulsive member of the human race today because of the injustice he has imposed on our Muslim nation." Then he added, "Today, the [Koran] has become his enemy. The Iranian nation has become his enemy."

While the shah continued to rule with an iron fist by controlling elections and shutting down the press, Khomeini continued preaching sermons and distributing leaflets condemning the shah. Finally, in November 1964, the shah had had enough and ordered Khomeini's exile to Turkey.

Age sixty-three when he left, Khomeini later settled in Najaf, Iraq, the theological center of Shia Islam, where it is believed that Ali (Mohammed's son-in-law) was murdered. He was now under the watchful eye of Iraq.

What the shah thought would silence his biggest critic and bring peace back to his torn nation only served to give Khomeini more freedom to spread his views of dissent among the Iranian people. Using mimeographs and audiocassettes, Khomeini had his sermons recorded and smuggled into the country where they were secretly distributed in mosques and on the streets. People wanted to know what this banished man had to say. The shah had created a much bigger problem.

The shah continued his crusade of unifying Iran through its pre-Islamic past. To celebrate Iran's twenty-five-hundred-year history, he ordered tents to be erected at Persepolis, one of the country's ancient capitals. He spared no expense, flying in more than one hundred fifty chefs from Paris, France, and spending an estimated $50 to $200 million. Khomeini received word of the excessive celebration and called anyone who attended the festivities a traitor to Islam and the Iranian people.

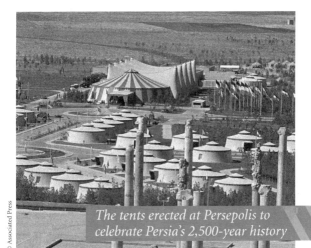

The tents erected at Persepolis to celebrate Persia's 2,500-year history

© Associated Press

In the meantime, oil quadrupled in price. The shah gave no price-break to the United States but used the money to build up his military. Tensions with the American presence in Iran grew. During Ashura, Americans insensitively used the Shia holiday to drink alcohol and carouse, blaring loud music. Muslims, who abstain from alcohol, were offended and angry, knowing they had no recourse with the Americans under SOFA.

What is most disturbing is that few people outside Iran knew the problems that were brewing. To them, the notion of Islam toppling the shah's government was unthinkable.

In a New Year's Eve celebration in Tehran, President Jimmy Carter, while on a tour to promote another peace initiative between the Arabs and Israel, toasted the shah, saying, "Iran under your leadership is an island of stability... This is a great tribute to you,... to the respect, admiration, and love which your people give to you." That island of stability was on shaky ground and would soon fall apart.

There was a growing rift between the rich and poor. The government was spending little money to modernize Iran. People were not embracing the shah's desire to link Iran to its pre-

Mohammed Reza Shah and Empress Farah in 1977

Islamic past. Instead, they were running to the mosques where they were finding meaning and purpose.

In a final gesture to silence Khomeini, the shah asked Iraqi president Saddam Hussein to send Khomeini to Paris, France,

where he would hopefully be disgraced into silence in the over-indulged, immoral West. Once again, the shah's plan backfired, and Paris proved to give Khomeini better access to communications and the media. Khomeini responded by ordering Iran's workers to strike, shutting down the nation and paralyzing the economy. The shah could not win. Even he could not stop the hypnotic effect that Khomeini had over the people. So in January 1979, the shah said good-bye to his country and took with him a small box of Iranian earth.

When he left, the country erupted into chaos. Mobs of vigilantes took to the streets raiding police stations and military bases, and even storming SAVAK (the shah's secret service) headquarters. Members of the shah's government were dragged into the street before makeshift courts and sentenced to death.

Two weeks after the shah had left, Khomeini arrived. On February 1, 1979, his Air France flight landed in Tehran national airport to mobs of Iranians holding placards of his portrait with the

Ayatollah Ruhollah Khomeni en route to Tehran on his Air France flight.

© Associated Press

caption "The Light of Our Life." Many cheered, *"Agha Amad!"* ("The respectful one has come"), and others wept at the return of the one whom they thought would save them from the "wiles" of the shah. He stepped off the plane and up to a microphone and declared, "This parliament and government are illegal. If they continue, we will arrest them. I will shut their mouths. And I will appoint a government with the support of the Iranian people."

From that moment on, Iran was never the same.

Khomeini's first order of business was ensuring Iran would become an Islamic state. He appointed a prime minister who wanted to give the people a choice between a religious or secular government. Khomeini refused, saying the only choice is to vote for or against a religious government. Ultimately, Iran voted ninety percent in favor of a religious government. The Islamic Republic of Iran was born. Khomeini responded that the election was "the first day of the government of God."

But it would not be long before his iron-fisted fury would be unleashed on the people and the church. Just weeks after Khomeini's arrival, activists took revenge on the church by cutting the throat of Reverend Aristou Sayyah, an Anglican priest.

Prior to the shah's departure, *komitehs* had formed in the mosques. They were made up of young men who acted as vigilante officers in defense of Khomeini's ideology. Somewhat reminiscent of Mao's Red Guards during the Cultural Revolution that cracked down on anything Western, the *komitehs* continued their zealous witch hunt after Khomeini's arrival, even barging into homes in search of alcohol. Mullahs shut down newspapers and Western movies, music, and other forms of entertainment. And the women were required to wear a veil.

Khomeini started the Revolutionary Council, a group of mullahs under his control that would later split off to become the Revolutionary Guard Corps (or *Pasdaran* in Persian), a military arm that can be described as a mix between an elite military unit and a mafia.

Unease spread among the people. In August 1979, leftists and liberals protested the new restrictions on the press. Khomeini immediately shouted them down with threats, saying, "When we want, we can throw you into a dustbin of death."

The country was only months away from voting on their new constitution, which would guarantee power to the mullahs. But with all the unrest, how would it pass? A month before the vote, students stormed the U.S. Embassy in Tehran and held the workers hostage. Though not instigated by Khomeini, he saw this as the answer to drum up support for the new constitution, saying anyone who did not support the constitution was a collaborator with the U.S. It worked. In December of that year, 99.5 percent of Iranians voted for the new constitution. But given the harsh crackdowns on free speech in the country, who would dare oppose it?

The following year, an attempt to rescue the embassy hostages had failed, when helicopters crashed in a sandstorm. Khomeini said the storm was God's way of protecting a nation governed by Islam, going so far as claiming that God threw sand at the helicopters.

As if vigilante justice were not enough, the government started the Center for the Campaign Against Sin, enforcing the way women dressed and ensuring that men grew beards. Ancient penalties for adultery were also reinstituted. Persecution of the church also increased. On May 6, 1980, Bahram Deghani-Tafti, the son of an Anglican bishop, was shot and killed. His father had survived an assassination attempt months earlier but fled to London. In some cities, authorities took over church-led hospitals and missionary houses.

More than a year after Khomeini's return, Saddam Hussein challenged the newly formed Islamic state by attacking its borders. But the war only served as an impetus to export the Islamic revolution to other nations, using martyrdom as a core military strategy.

IRAN TODAY:
"JESUS CAME TO ME"

The Voice of the Martyrs interviewed a woman named Jilla, who shared how she came to know Jesus and the challenges she faced in growing in Christ as a Muslim-background believer in Iran. Following is a portion of her testimony, adapted from the book Desperate for God.

In the sixth grade, I became a *Basiege*—a girl who is dedicated to Islam, almost like a military-style worship. In school I would take the microphone and sing mournfully like in a funeral service, almost as if the prophet Hussein (Mohammed's grandson) had just died, although he died thousands of years ago. Then we hit ourselves. I would hit myself harder than everybody else and would bleed. In school they taught me that whoever would fast the longest would have a more secure place in heaven. I did that for such a long time that once I ended up in the hospital.

We were flooded with all kinds of spiritual laws. Because I was the *Basiege* leader for three years, the girls at school would all look to me to lead them in prayer. Everybody had to pray, especially during the month of Hussein [the holiday called Ashura].

The Muslim prophet Hussein's grave is in Iraq. We remember his martyrdom around October. Every year at this time a dark spirit would come over me. Under Islam I was always grieving. When I would feel like this, my peace would leave. I thought this was my fault because I'm such a horrible sinner.

I would pray five different times from early morning until late at night. I would bow 400 times in four different directions. When I woke up in the morning, my knees would hurt.

In the mosque I had to stand behind a huge curtain in the middle, dividing the men from the women. The women are all behind the black curtain. The women can only hear the mullah's voice from the microphone, but we cannot see him. We can only listen and repeat the prayers aloud, kneeling on the carpet while bowing over and over.

Many of the women needing spiritual or emotional help make an appointment with the mullah for counseling. He sees them and wants them sexually, calling them "temporary wives," so women very rarely see him.

Even with my religious zeal, I knew these things were wrong and continued to search for goodness.

During this time of my life, one of my sisters came back from college to our small town and brought a movie with her. It was the life of Christ according to Luke. I went to a room of our house where we all watch TV. I just happened to be alone and put the movie in. While watching how Jesus loved people, I began to cry. At the end of the film, there was a prayer of repentance. I prayed it six times. I don't think I realized what repentance meant, but I wanted to be near to God.

I automatically went on my knees and started lifting up my hands. I was always jealous of my sister after she came back from college because she would kneel down and without any Muslim beads or clothes or holy stones, she would lift up her hands and start praying.

I thought, *Well, this is it. This is what I am looking for.* I began to pray in Farsi that I would be delivered from sin. It was like God was talking to me. He was saying, "This is the truth. I am the true God. I am the one God." I ran into the kitchen and found my saved sister. I just had to tell her.

My sister threw her hands up and said, "I don't know what to tell you. I don't have any teaching yet."

I didn't have my own Bible yet. All I had was a colored picture of Jesus about six inches tall. To feel close to Him, I would pull my sleeping mat over and sit on the side He was looking at. I felt He was fathering me and loving me through that picture.

Later, Christians led [my sister and me] to a home group of five or six Christians who had left Islam. Our names are Muslim, not Armenian. The authorities do not like us to attend a church, and culturally we are somewhat different. So the home group was good for our physical and spiritual security.

Finally, I got my own New Testament from my group leader. I was so happy. In Iran, Christians or curious Muslims must travel hundreds of miles to find one. The Bible Society was closed after 1979, when we became an Islamic Republic.

We're all learning to understand how the apostle Paul had to suffer things and what this felt like. When our Christian friends tell us these things happen, we want to share the pain with them. We read about Paul together and pray with them. If we feel it's going to be really dangerous, we start fasting.

Within six weeks of seeing the film about Jesus, I started sharing on the bus. In the morning on the bus ride to work, I would witness to two or three people and again in the evening on my way home.

Although I went to a church, they never said anything about sharing your faith. Perhaps they are afraid of the government. But at one point, I realized I've been freed of so many things, and these people in Iran are in the same sort of prison that I was in. I must share with them what released me.

In Iran, there are chat rooms just for people from their areas. The authorities trace e-mails, but not chats. They also track text messaging, trying to find us. I witnessed one time to people in India; three of them wanted to receive the Lord. I also shared with some in England.

I am twenty years old and have been a Christian two years.

I always wanted to get to Christ with my own efforts. But when I finally got to the point where I was so broken, that's when Jesus came to me.

MARTYRDOM AS A STRATEGY: EXPORTING THE REVOLUTION (1980–1990)

They were promised immediate entry into paradise if they died on the battlefield. With a key around their neck that would open the door to paradise, they chanted, *"Allahu Akhbar!"* ("Allah is the greatest!") and went to their deaths. These were Iran's *Basiji* (or *Basiege*).

Khomeini's Iran was losing the war with Saddam Hussein's Iraq, and Khomeini was desperate to do something. What he chose was not just extreme. It was homicidal, if not insane.

Embracing the Shia's fixation with martyrdom rooted in the death of Hussein in the seventh century, Khomeini sent teenage boys to charge

Outside Tehran, female members of Iran's Basij at a training session at a Revolutionary Guards base

© Reuters

the frontlines, detonating land mines as they ran toward their Iraqi enemies. Often recruited at school, having not even said good-bye to their childhood, these *Basiji* (members of the *Basij*) responded to Khomeini's call to the higher good: martyrdom for the cause of Iran. Few survived.

Today, the *Basiji* are present in almost every city in Iran and answer to the Iranian Revolutionary Guards. They no longer storm the frontlines of battle, using their bodies as detonators, but perform public service acts such as community organizing, policing morals, and suppressing protests.

Since childhood, the Shia Muslim is indoctrinated to "feel the great historic wrong committed against the Shia by the Sunnis and to accept as their task the recapture of Karbala"[8] (located in present-day Iraq) from the Sunnis. That desire for revenge has been passed down from fathers to sons for centuries. And it became one of Khomeini's greatest weapons as he exported the Islamic Revolution to nearby countries. As one expert has stated, "For Iran, the suicide bomber is part of its military arsenal, a tool with a tactical military purpose."[9]

Expanding Khomeini's Influence

Throughout the 1980s, Khomeini plotted to spread Shia influence across the Muslim world in

8 Mackey, p. 319.

9 Baer, p. 205.

an effort to control it, while attempting to undermine the West's (especially the United States') presence and sway in the Middle East. In what could be called a "new Islamic world order," Khomeini and the clerics wrote a new constitution declaring, "All Muslims shall be considered as one single nation and the Islamic Republic of Iran shall make its general policy on the basis of coalition and unity of all Muslim people and shall constantly make every endeavor to realize the political, economic and cultural unity of the world of Islam."[10]

He began his "new Islamic world order" by focusing on inflaming Shia populations in nearby Arab states. But he set his sights beyond the Shia population. Through the chaos and discontent that he would provoke, he hoped to rally to his cause both Shia and Sunnis who had felt oppressed by their governments. He started in 1981 by targeting the sheikh of the small island of Bahrain, whose Shia population was sixty percent. The plot to overthrow the sheikh was discovered, and Iran made no apologies. They then turned their focus to Kuwait (thirty percent Shia), where they set off six bombs, killing six and injuring eighty, while damaging the embassies of two of its Western enemies: America and France. Although Iran did not publicly take responsibility for the attack, many felt its presence behind it.

---

10 Mackey, pp. 309,310.

Lebanon was another battlefield for Khomeini's Islamic ideology. Outside Iran, Lebanon has the largest number of Shia Muslims in the world. When Israel attacked Lebanon in 1982, Iran stepped in to help the Lebanese Shia. But this time, Iran was smarter. It used proxies, such as the terrorist groups Hezbollah and the elusive Islamic Jihad, to do its dirty work, including bombing of the American Embassy compound in Beirut in April 1983 and the Marine barracks the following October, killing two hundred forty-one U.S. Marines. When Israel pulled out of Lebanon years later, Iran viewed it as a victory.

Though Khomeini shifted his focus outside Iran's borders, trouble still remained for the church. Between 1979 and 1985, about a half dozen church leaders were assassinated or executed.

Khomeini soon shifted his attention to the *Hajj* (the pilgrimage to Mecca, Saudi Arabia—one of the five tenets of Islam). He sent more than one hundred fifty thousand Iranian Shia to the *Hajj*. Thousands of Iranians spilled into the street with posters proclaiming "Victory is made by waves of martyrs." In a clash with Saudi police, more than four hundred Iranians were killed. Khomeini was immediately charged with trying to declare himself the leader of the Muslim world. Khomeini did not deny it: "We will export our experiences to the whole world...This exportation will certainly result in the blooming of the buds of victory and independence and in the implementation of Islamic teachings among en-slaved nations."

However, with Iraq, Iran was not so success-ful. Iran's inflation rate was soaring, and the war with Iraq was draining its treasury. As a final blow of defeat, in July 1988 Khomeini finally gave in and accepted the United Nations cease-fire resolution that had been presented the previ-ous year. However, two days later he told Iran that he would have preferred "death and martyr-dom," but accepted the agreement "in the interest of the Islamic Republic."

But Iran would not cease to support its prox-ies—Hezbollah, Hamas, and Islamic Jihad—and would later be considered the world's largest fin-ancier of terrorism.

Khomeini left a legacy of martyrdom as a military strategy in promoting his Islamic world-view. But soon after his death in 1989, a different kind of martyr would appear—one that would not take the lives of others but would bear wit-ness to a life far greater than any ayatollah.

CHRISTIANITY UNDER FIRE: A SERIES OF MARTYRDOMS (1990-1996)

Some were church leaders. Some were Muslim-background believers. But all five who were killed were connected in some way. The reign of Ayatollah Ruhollah Khomeini had come to an end with his death on June 3, 1989. Although he was gone, Iran was still ruled with the Koran gripped in an iron fist, even slamming the doors to the Iranian Bible Society in 1979, which had been opened by the Russian Bible Society in 1816.

Though only one of these five Christians was killed at the hands of an Iranian court, the others' deaths seemed suspicious. Were these deaths intended to keep cases of "religious persecution" off the Iranian government's already poor human-rights record? Were they part of the government's unofficial campaign to silence and intimidate the church? Or were they meant to send a clear message to any Muslim who dared to consider leaving Islam? And would it work?

"Sanctioned" and "Non-Sanctioned" Executions

He left Islam when he was thirteen, and for this, he became a marked man. Pastor of the Assemblies of God church in Mashhad, Reverend Hussein Soodmand was arrested as an apostate decades after his conversion.

He was held for one month and then re-leased. His family, relieved, thought the ordeal was over. Six months later he was rearrested. But this time, the authorities brought his case to an end once and for all.

Given a choice to deny his faith and give up his church or face death, he refused to deny the One who gave him eternal life. "He could not renounce his God," recalled his daughter in an interview. "His belief in Christ was his life—it was his deepest conviction."

He was tried in a Shariah (Islamic) court where he was found guilty of apostasy and sentenced to death by hanging. On December 3, 1990, Reverend Soodmand left this world and met his Creator face to face.

As of this writing, Reverend Soodmand was the last known judicially sanctioned execution of an apostate. The other four men faced non-sanctioned executions either for their apostasies, for their leadership in the church, or for their actions to tell the world of the plight of Iranian Christians.

Born into a Muslim family, Mehdi Dibaj committed an unpardonable sin in the mind of Muslims when he committed his life to Christ. Iranian law caught up with him in the early 1980s when he was arrested and held without trial. Adding to his torment, his wife, threatened with stoning, divorced him and returned to Islam. After nine years in prison, Dibaj was convicted of apostasy in December 1993 and condemned to die. In his defense, he seized the opportunity to preach the gospel. (See the sidebar on page 88.)

Outraged by Dibaj's death sentence, Bishop Haik Hovsepian had to act. Leader of an Armenian church in Iran, Bishop Haik decided to tell the world about Dibaj's case, hoping that would cause authorities to overturn his death sentence. But he knew that came with a risk. "If we go to jail or die for our

Bishop Haik Hovsepian-Mehr, martyred in 1994

faith," he shared, "we want the whole Christian world to know what is happening to their Christian brothers and sisters."

On January 16, 1994, Haik's efforts paid off. Dibaj was released. But just three days later, Haik disappeared off the streets. Weeks passed before authorities finally reported Haik's death to his family.

Five months later, Dibaj faced the same end. On his way to celebrate his daughter's birthday, he was abducted and killed.

But the killings were not over.

Reverend Tateos Michaelian had just taken Bishop Haik's position as Chairman of the Protestant Council of Ministers in 1994, when he, too, was targeted. He was found dead in Tehran, having been shot sometime between June 29 and July 2. Considered Iran's leading Christian translator, Michaelian left a considerable gap in the Christian community. Like his Nestorian predecessors during the Great Persecution of the fourth century, taking on this leadership position was a death sentence. But one more martyr was yet to join the ranks.

Under the ministry of Reverend Hussein Soodmand, Mohammed Bajher Yusefi left Islam for Christianity at the age of 24. A very gifted evangelist, Yusefi became pastor of the Assemblies of God churches in Mazandaran and became known as "Ravanbaksh," meaning "soulgiver." During part of Dibaj's time in prison, Yusefi and his wife cared for Dibaj's sons.

Mohammed Bajher Yusefi, martyred in 1996

On September 28, 1996, Yusefi left his home in Sari at six o'clock in the morning and never returned. Later that night, his family was notified that his body had been found hanging in a tree.

What was meant to silence and intimidate the church—especially Muslim converts to Christianity—proved to do the opposite. The martyrdoms not only drew the attention of more Iranians to the gospel, but drew the attention of the world to the treatment of Christians in Iran. The number of conversions from Islam to Christianity continued to grow.

As Iran's message of hate and support of terror increased in the next decade, many Muslims would find the hope of Christ in the "axis of evil."

EXCERPTS FROM
MEHDI DIBAJ'S DEFENSE

He was sentenced to die. His wife had left him. Having already spent nine years in prison, Mehdi Dibaj was not without hope or courage. He used his defense to share the gospel with those who had gathered for his trial. Here are excerpts from his defense given in December 1993, before the Sari Court of Justice, bearing witness to his tremendous faith in the face of death.

I would rather have the whole world against me, but know that the Almighty God is with me. I would rather be called an apostate, but know that I have the approval of the God of glory, because man looks at the outward appearance but God looks at the heart. For Him who is God for all eternity, nothing is impossible. All power in heaven and on earth is in His hands.

They tell me, "Return!" but to whom can I return from the arms of my God? Is it right to accept what people are saying instead of obeying the Word of God? It is now forty-five years that I am walking with the God of miracles, and His kindness upon me is like a shadow and I owe Him much for His fatherly love and concern.

The God of Daniel, who protected his friends in the fiery furnace, has protected me for nine years in prison. And all the bad happenings have turned out for our good and gain, so much so that I am filled to overflowing with joy and thankfulness.

The God of Job has tested my faith and commitment in order to increase my patience and faithfulness. During these nine years, He has freed me from all my responsibilities so that under the protection of His blessed name, I would spend my time in prayer and study of His Word...I praise God for this unique opportunity. God gave me space in my confinement, brought healing in my difficult hardships, and His kindness revived me. Oh, what great blessings God has in store for those who fear Him!

[Jesus] is our Savior and He is the Son of God. To know Him means to know eternal life. I, a useless sinner, have believed in this beloved Person and all His words and miracles recorded in the Gospel, and I have commit-

Mehdi Dibaj,
martyred in 1994

ted my life into His hands. Life for me is an opportunity to serve Him, and death is a better opportunity to be with Christ. Therefore I am not only satisfied to be in prison for the honor of His holy name, but am ready to give my life for the sake of Jesus, my Lord, and enter His kingdom sooner, the place where the elect of God enter everlasting life.

WORDS OF HOPE FROM CHRISTIANS IN IRAN TODAY

"Our group takes Bibles home to give to new converts, but the shortage of Bibles is a big problem. We pray to get more Bibles. One worship group has been under attack. The government spies are pretty active and some of our group members have been under interrogation. With many prayers, nothing has happened to the members. The great news about our groups is they are growing despite pressure. Our group members get daring in hard times."

—AN ANONYMOUS IRANIAN CHRISTIAN MAN

"We must move every two or three years. This is the seventh place we have moved to in thirteen years, yet this is not important. We don't want any home here because we know where our home is. We are always ready to go to our main home with Jesus. I'm not afraid of death because I know where I am going."

—DR. "G" ON THE DIFFICULTIES HE AND HIS WIFE FACE FOR PREACHING THE GOSPEL IN IRAN

"This third generation (generation after 1979)—no one believes in Islam. They are against what is gong on in Iran, the fanaticism. I tell them about Christ and some say Christianity is harder than Islam because it demands a lot. I tell them no, Christ is easy to receive and the difficulty is in Islam, not Christianity. Most want to become Christian, but the problem is fear.

"They're afraid because they could be killed. If they have no faith, they won't be bothered. I know the risk of going to prison or being killed, yet I'm ready to face the challenge."

—"RASHID," A TAXICAB DRIVER IN IRAN, WHO RISKS HIS LIFE TELLING OTHERS ABOUT JESUS

"Life is difficult, just living—the pressures are terrible. I have Jesus Christ, so I'm not afraid. God is testing our faith because He wants it to grow so that we become more like Jesus. So much blood has been shed for our faith. The resurrection power of Jesus gives us strength to carry on."

—"NOOR," A HOUSE CHURCH LEADER IN IRAN

"Christianity is growing in Iran because Islam is like a melon, a melon that wasn't yet opened. When it started being opened, people discover what is inside. In Iran, sometimes the melon is not always red inside. Sometimes it can be white. That is why I used this example, because the melon is not always red. It may look nice and round, but when you just cut it, when you take it home, you realize sometimes it is red, sometimes it is not. They realize that Islam was not really that nice red, juicy thing inside."

—"GHODSI," A WOMAN WHO CONVERTED FROM ISLAM TO CHRISTIANITY

FINDING HOPE IN THE RHETORIC OF HATE (21ST CENTURY)

The iron-fisted leadership of Ayatollah Ruhollah Khomeini backfired. Fed up with the cultural restrictions imposed by the Islamic Revolution, many Iranians were tired of the anti-American, anti-Israel, anti-West rhetoric, forcing them to ask themselves, *Is this all there is?* Thus began their journey toward hope.

As Iran transitioned into the twenty-first century, its government structure and tactics shifted, though its message of fanaticism did not. Once called a theocracy, Iran is believed to be more of a military state, making policy decisions on the basis of Shia Islamic principles. One expert believes that mullahs gave up the "Koran for the Kalashnikov" (an assault rifle)—that is, their aim is less religious and more military/political. The president of the country has very little executive authority. The authority lies with the Supreme Leader but not entirely. The Guardian Council must approve laws passed in the *Majlis*. At the time of writing, the Supreme Leader is Ayatollah Ali Khameini, who is described as being "part cleric, part mediator, part dictator, part military commander and part police chief."[11]

While Iran tried to modernize, its image still did not improve among world leaders. Former

---

11 Baer, p. 127.

Secretary of State Warren Christopher called the country an "outlaw state," and President George W. Bush referred to Iran as part of an "axis of evil." Others have confirmed that Iran continues as the world's largest exporter of terrorism. Likewise, Iran's newly elected president, Mahmoud Ahmadinejad, did not help matters when he claimed that the Holocaust never happened and that Israel should be wiped off the face of the earth.

It was simply more of the same: the ominous, fanatical figure of Ayatollah Ruhollah Khomeini's Islamic Revolution hovering over the nation.

But there is more to this story—more hope.

Because of Iran's rhetoric of hate, its citizens are looking for hope, and they are finding it in the Person of Jesus Christ. Christians are sharing Christ on busses and in taxis, in schools, and in the workplace, knowing that if caught, they will be dealt with severely. Refusing to remain silent and marginalized as their Nestorian predecessors were, many Iranian Christians are risking prison and death by sharing the hope of Christ with Muslims who are tired of the hate-filled zealotry of Khomeini's revolution.

In a November 2005 meeting of thirty provincial governors, Ahmadinejad vowed to end the growing movement of house churches in the country. Yet the following year, he noted that five to six hundred Muslims were converting to Christianity *every month*—a number some believe is underestimated.

Risking All to Share the Hope

Though it is considered legal to be a Christian in Iran, those who lead a Muslim to Christ have faced severe penalties. And Muslims who choose to abandon their faith in exchange for Christ (Muslim-Background Believers, or MBBs) are not exempt either.

Iranian secret police have raided the dorm rooms of Christian students, confiscating New Testaments, Christian booklets, gospel CDs, and videos about Jesus, and then hauling the students off to prison. Once they are released, their fellow students only want to know more about their "crime," which opens doors to share the gospel.

And those Muslims who respond to the gospel, such as Hamid Pourmand, pay dearly.

© Compass Direct

Hamid Pourmand with his family

In February 2005, a military tribunal in Tehran found Hamid guilty of deceiving the Iranian army by concealing his conversion from Islam to Christianity, and sentenced him to prison. Hamid was a lay pastor who openly spoke of his newfound faith with his friends, family, and Muslim converts to Christ. After Christians around the world pleaded for his case, he was released fourteen months early. Now Iran has threatened Hamid to stay quiet about his faith, warning him that his release orders could be revoked if he attends church.

Some Christians have been sent into the arms of Christ much sooner, like Abbas Amiri. A veteran of the Iran-Iraq War and honored pilgrim of the Islamic *Hajj*, Abbas had enough of Islam and converted to Christianity. Police were furious. In July 2008, they raided his home, then arrested and brutally beat him. He was hospitalized and died less than two weeks later. His widow died just four days after her husband was buried.

Even conducting Bible studies with Muslims will reveal the harsh face of Iran's government.

Having become new converts to Christ, Tina Rad and her husband, Makan Arya, were arrested for holding a Bible study with Muslims. Charged with "activities against national security," Makan was beaten severely. Tina was charged with "activities against the holy religion of Islam." Her face and body were badly bruised from the beating she received. Authorities threatened the couple with prison and told them they would lose their daughter if they did not cooperate. They were forced to sign a statement promising they would not attend house church meetings or make contact with other Christians. While Tina was in custody, a female security officer told her that the next time she would be charged with apostasy "if you don't stop with your Jesus."

Tina Rad

© Compass Direct

These Muslim-background believers cannot "stop with their Jesus" when He has given them eternal life and hope amid so much evil and hate in their country.

In an effort to stop Muslim conversions to Christ, in 2008 the Iranian parliament (*Majlis*) passed a new draft of the Islamic Penal Code, which would mandate the death sentence for any male convicted of leaving Islam. A woman would face life in prison. Almost two hundred voted in favor of the bill, with only seven voting against it. At the time of this writing, the bill had passed parliament but is awaiting review by the Council of Mullahs before it becomes law. Judicially sanctioned executions could become the norm in Iran, but another concern is those who have already converted to Christianity and are in jail for apostasy. How will the law affect them? Ultimately, will the law successfully silence the church? Or will it serve to reinforce the zealous hatred that came with Ayatollah Ruhollah Khomeini's ideal of a pure Islamic state?

There is more hope for Iranians.

With the increasing availability of satellite dishes, Christians have been tuning in to an Iranian Christian broadcast. Thousands of Iranians are watching this program produced by International Antioch Ministries (IAM). As a result, many Iranians have come to Christ. "Every day, we get calls from Iran from people who report that their lives have been changed," shared Dr. Hormoz Shariat, president of IAM. "They have been set free from addictions, and their families have been restored. We are making a positive difference in Iran and are saving lives." And IAM isn't the only ministry producing such Christian broadcasts in Iran. There are others. They offer hope in a country that has one of the world's highest percentages of drug addicts, according to news agencies that began reporting such information in 2006.

Iranians are able to call IAM in response to the satellite broadcast. They ask for prayer and for more Bible verses to be voiced over the air. Some callers have threatened to harm IAM workers. Contacts with The Voice of the Martyrs say that Iran recently passed a law targeting those living outside Iran who "are actively trying to weaken Islam"—singling out people like Dr. Hormoz, who work through television and the Internet. The new law promises to convict even those who do not live in the country. Punishment includes death.

One in four households owns a satellite dish, though they are officially banned. Police have smashed satellite dishes to curtail the West's influence, but Iranians still take the risk, sometimes covering their dishes with blankets to conceal them from authorities. Perhaps knowing the success of Ayatollah Ruhollah Khomeini's campaign in exile—distributing pamphlets, mimeographs, and cassettes to spread his revolutionary ideology —has Iran worried. Perhaps Iran is just using a tactic that has worked in the past: unifying the people under a banner of hate by shifting the

Iranians sometimes cover their satellite dishes with blankets to conceal them from authorities.

country's focus onto a common enemy—this time, apostates.

Unless Christians decide to remain quiet and keep their faith to themselves, the church in Iran will continue growing. Their examples have been lived out; their heroes are in place. They have modern-day models of courage in the face of death—Bishop Haik, Pastor Yusefi, Mehdi Dibaj, and others who have given their lives for the gospel. Iranians are receiving Scriptures in their own language (Farsi) and stories of Christians who have been persecuted for the faith to encourage and strengthen them in times of peril. And they have the Body of Christ around the world to stand with them in prayer as we look to the road ahead for the church in Iran.

IRAN TODAY:
HOPE THROUGH THE AIRWAVES

The Voice of the Martyrs helps support the satellite programs that International Antioch Ministries airs six nights a week in Iran. Here are excerpts of two testimonies from individuals who have found the hope of Christ through the broadcast.

I came to know Jesus through your programs and now that I have a Bible, I am reading it every day. I pray that God will answer your prayer and my prayer and change the situation in Iran so that we can have a church in Mashad where we all can worship the true God without fear. Sometimes I go to the only church building in Mashad and look at it. Seeing it vacant and abandoned makes me cry. With tearful eyes, I often pray that God will give my greatest wish and open the door of this church soon. Every month, I set aside the tithe of my income in a special account so that some day I will have a part in re-opening of this church building.

I watch your programs every night. Last night when you mentioned that you and your church are paying $70,000 for air time every year, it touched me deeply. It is through your programs that we are taught and we grow in Christ. You know in Iran we do not have a place to go for teaching. I want to thank you and all who contribute to this program because they are min-

istering to me and people like me and causing
the Word of God to go forth and help people like
me, who are thirsty for the truth, to grow in our
faith.

So please tell the believers in your church
publicly. Thank each believer on behalf of new
believers like me because they are supporting
your TV program so that we can see your programs every night. Tell them: "You do not know
how greatly you are ministering to us. May the
Lord bless you."

If possible, please increase the number of
hours of your programs.

—A MAN FROM THE CITY OF MASHAD

I came to believe Jesus through your programs
several months ago. I kept watching your programs but I did not dare share the news with my
husband. He was a fanatical Muslim. I knew that
if he found out that I had become a Christian, he
would divorce me. So I kept my mouth shut for
several months.

When Ramadan started, I did not know what
to do. If I fasted, I would feel that I am denying
Christ and going back to my Islamic faith. If I did
not fast, my husband would ask me why and
would find out about my faith. Thank God I
called you for advice. You told me to fast but fast
and pray for the salvation of my husband. So I
fasted but all day I prayed that my husband would
be attracted to Jesus.

IRAN

On the third day of Ramadan, my husband and I were watching your program. In the middle of your program, my husband turned to me and said, "You know, I want to follow Jesus. From tonight on, I will not fast for Ramadan and will not pray. From now on I am not following Islam but Jesus." He then turned to me and said, "How about you?" It was then that I joyfully shared with him that I had taken that step several months before.

Now my husband and I are both believers and watch your programs every day.

—A WOMAN FROM THE CITY OF TEHRAN

THE ROAD AHEAD:
PRAY FOR IRAN

The Persian queen knew she was risking her life. Queen Esther had just learned that Haman, the king's royal adviser, had convinced the king to annihilate her people, the Jews. Her uncle, Mordecai, sent her a message that she could be their only hope. Still, she argued with him. She hadn't been called to see the king, and approaching him unrequested could cost her life.

"Don't think that being in the king's palace will protect you," her uncle responded. "God may raise up another deliverer in your place, but you will surely perish. Perhaps you were appointed for such a time as this."

Finally, she was convinced and called for a fast. "If I perish, I perish," she responded.

She put on her royal robe and stood before the inner court with the king in view. Her eyes locked on every movement of the golden scepter that he gripped. If it remained motionless, her life was over.

As soon as the king saw his beautiful queen, he held out the scepter allowing her to approach. But her task was not complete.

After inviting the king and Haman to a banquet but failing to confront the scheming adviser, she invited them to yet another. Finally, the king asked her, "What is it that you wanted, Queen?"

Knowing Haman's influence over the king and what was at stake, she knew the risk to her people was far greater than the risk to her own life, so she told him of Haman's plan for mass genocide.

The gallows Haman had constructed on which to execute Esther's uncle was instead used to hang him. Esther's people were saved.

* * *

The situation is not much different in Persia today. In modern-day Iran, "Hamans" are still trying to put an end to the church. Yet the King we serve is one whose "throne of grace" we can freely approach in time of need (Hebrews 4:16). We can tell Him about the Hamans of the world, asking for courage, mercy, and protection for our persecuted brothers and sisters in Christ in Iran who, much like Esther, take great risks to share the gospel of hope in the "axis of evil."

We can pray that God will continue to embolden and empower believers in Iran to tell others about Jesus on busses, in taxis, and in the classroom. We can ask Him to use satellite broadcasts to continue opening the hardened hearts of Muslims to the message of eternal life through Christ. We can pray that He will get Bibles and other Christian literature into the hands of believers so they can grow in Him. And we can pray for salvation for Iran's leaders—the ayatollahs, the mullahs, the clerics, the president, and other government officials.

Many of Iran's Christians have likewise said, "If I perish, I perish," as they risked prison or death for turning away from Islam or for leading other Muslims to Christ. Knowing that Muslims will perish eternally is far more important than their own temporal survival.

Their Nestorian predecessors had chosen the path of survival under the Zoroastrians and the invading Arab Muslims from the south. Marginal-

Iran today

ized in their own community, they were given the illusion of freedom and authority. Over time they lost the ability to read and write their ancient language, so they were unable to learn from the Scriptures and other literature left behind by fellow Nestorians, many of whom had faced death for their faith.

But today, many Iranian Christians refuse to be marginalized. Some pastors refuse to preach in their native Armenian. Instead, they risk all by preaching in Farsi, knowing that Muslims seeking Christ find their way into their pews. And those Muslim-background believers are refusing to remain quiet about Christ.

We can continue to be a part of their ministry as we choose to petition our King, Jesus Christ. But the question comes down to you: Will you pray for Iran? We need not fear His golden scepter, so what are you waiting for?

Hope is being found in the "axis of evil." Will you be a part of it? It's not too late to go before our King at "such a time as this." It's why you were appointed. Perhaps it's *your* time. Will you?

FOR FURTHER READING

The following books and resources were consulted in the writing of this book. However, The Voice of the Martyrs and the author do not necessarily share all the views presented in these resources.

Baer, Robert. *The Devil We Know: Dealing With the New Iranian Superpower* (New York: Crown Publishers, 2008).

Fahlbusch, Erwin and Geoffrey William Bromiley. *The Encyclopedia of Christianity* (Grand Rapids, MI: Wm. B. Eerdman's Publishing Company, 2001).

Hefley, James and Marti. *By Their Blood* (Grand Rapids, MI: Baker Books, 1996).

January, Brendan. *The Iranian Revolution* (Minneapolis: Twenty-First Century Books, 2008).

Mackey, Sandra. *The Iranians: Persia, Islam and the Soul of a Nation* (New York: Dutton, The Penguin Group, 1996).

Moffett, Samuel Hugh. *A History of Christianity in Asia, Volume I: Beginnings to 1500* (Maryknoll, NY: Orbis Books, 1998).

Moffett, Samuel Hugh. *A History of Christianity in Asia, Volume II: 1500 to 1900* (Maryknoll, NY: Orbis Books, 2005).

Richter, Julius, D. D. *A History of Protestant Missions in the Near East* (New York: Fleming H. Revell Company, 1910).

The Voice of the Martyrs. *Desperate for God* (Bartlesville, OK: Living Sacrifice Book Company, 2006).

Water, Mark, compiler. *The New Encyclopedia of Christian Martyrs* (Grand Rapids, MI: Baker Books, 2001).

Ye'or, Bat. *The Decline of Eastern Christianity under Islam: From Jihad to Dhimmitude* (Cranbury, NJ: Fairleigh Dickinson University Press, 1996).

Other Resources

The Voice of the Martyrs: www.persecution.com

The Voice of the Martyrs monthly newsletter

International Antioch Ministries: www.iam-online.net

RESOURCES

The Voice of the Martyrs has many books, videos, brochures, and other products to help you learn more about the persecuted church. In the U.S., to order materials or receive our free monthly newsletter, call (800) 747-0085 or write to:

The Voice of the Martyrs
P.O. Box 443
Bartlesville, OK 74005-0443
www.persecution.com
thevoice@vom-usa.org

If you are in Australia, Canada, New Zealand, South Africa, or the United Kingdom, contact:

Australia:
Voice of the Martyrs
P.O. Box 250
Lawson NSW 2783
Australia

Website: www.persecution.com.au
Email: thevoice@persecution.com.au

Canada:
Voice of the Martyrs, Inc.
P.O. Box 608
Streetsville, ON L5M 2C1
Canada

Website: www.persecution.net
Email: thevoice@vomcanada.org

New Zealand:

    Voice of the Martyrs
    P.O. Box 5482
    Papanui, Christchurch 8542
    New Zealand

    Website: www.persecution.co.nz
    Email: thevoice@persecution.co.nz

South Africa:

    Christian Mission International
    P.O. Box 7157
    1417 Primrose Hill
    South Africa

    Email: cmi@icon.co.za

United Kingdom:

    Release International
    P.O. Box 54
    Orpington BR5 9RT
    United Kingdom

    Website: www.releaseinternational.org
    Email: info@releaseinternational.org